Godz Girl
Inspire One
25 DAY DEVOTIONAL

YOLANDA
FLEMING-WILLIAMS

Copyright © 2025 by Yolanda Fleming-Williams

All rights reserved. No part of this book may be reproduced, stored in a retrieval system, or transmitted in any form or by any means—electronic, mechanical, photocopying, recording, or otherwise—without the prior written permission of the publisher, except in the case of brief quotations embodied in critical reviews and certain other noncommercial uses permitted by copyright law. Published by Writing in Faith

Iamwritinginfaith.com
Printed in the United States of America

ISBN: 979-8-9889051-4-1

First Edition: 2025

For permission requests, inquiries, or bulk orders, contact: godzgirlinspireone@gmail.com

Unless otherwise noted, all Scripture quotations are taken from the King James Version (KJV) of the Bible. Public domain.

Contents

Contents	3
Dedication	5
A Circle of Blessings	7
My Mama Was Two-Sided	13
What If...	17
God is... Our Who Dat!!	21
We Belong	25
Poor Little Rich Girl	29
Always Something...	33
Now I Know...	39
Always a Way Back	43
High as a Kite...	47
It's Okay to... BE-the-WORD	53
In Moments Like These	57
Knock, Knock, Knock	61
You Have Your Mother's Strength...	65
I Promise I Won't Be Long...	69
The Good New Days...	73

I Can Care Less...	77
I'll Take the Leftovers...	81
Sorry, We're Closed...	85
I Had No Clue...	89
GodzGirl InspireOne...	93
Red Means Go... and Break the Rules...	98
Dress Accordingly...	103
For Mature Adults Only...	107
There's a New Dance in Town...	111
Author Contact Page	116

Dedication

To **GodzGirls** everywhere—

This book is dedicated to you, the strong, the resilient, the broken, and the healed. To the women who have walked through fire and come out refined, who have stumbled yet risen stronger, who have fought silent battles and still choose to love, serve, and inspire.

May you always remember that **you are chosen, you are loved, and you are never alone.**

To the **GodzGirl** in you—may you continue to walk boldly in your purpose, unapologetically shining the light of God's love.

And above all, this is dedicated to the One who makes all things possible — **to God, my rock, my redeemer, my strength, and my guide.**

May His love be the anthem of your life, and may you forever inspire one.

A Circle of Blessings

I forgot to tell y'all:
Going around in circles; not so bad...

We all have heard the song *"You Got Me Going in Circles, Round and Round I Go,"* right?

Most dictionaries say going around in circles means not achieving anything because you keep coming back to the same point or problem. On one hand, that is true in some matters. But what if I told you there is a type of circling that brings **JOY, HOPE, and an increase in FAITH?**

Lately, in my own life, I've been circling around people from my past. I'm pretty sure we all have met people who just felt kindred—not related to you naturally, but spiritually, there is an unexplainable connection. God has a funny way of having people circle around in our lives, and we don't know why at the time.

Years ago, I met a young lady, and we made a great connection. Although I can't recall all of our conversations and whatnots, I had developed a connection with her outside of the normal, natural connection. We hadn't spoken to one another since those years ago, but recently, she made a post on Facebook, and I immediately responded—not knowing that my response would cause us to reconnect.

Later that evening, she responded back to me, and the question she asked would change my thoughts on something as simple as a circle. The young lady asked me if I would be able to watch her 3.5-month-old baby. At first, I smiled and was in wonder all at the same time. Like I said, we had not spoken or physically seen each other in years. But God has a way of making a circle of blessings. So, of course, I said yes—I would love to watch your little one. He would stay the night while Mom went to work. I was elated that she had so much trust in me that she would allow me to care for her most precious gift—her child.

Little did I know, I needed this experience, and I didn't even realize it at the time of my response to her Facebook post.

This baby was like no other child I had ever cared for before. At 3.5 months, he had such a **PEACE** about him that I just wanted to hold him close and cover him from anything and everything that would even try to disturb him in any way. I knew something was very special about this beautiful, peaceful baby boy because my sixteen-year-old daughter asked if she could hold him—and she never asks to hold anyone's baby. But this baby was different.

In those little moments he stayed with us, we realized that even when the world says going around in circles leads to no achievement—

only problems with no solutions—
experiencing the PEACE of this
little baby boy taught us that God
can demonstrate His LOVE and His
PEACE in so many ways. I'm so
glad He gave me and my family an
opportunity to feel His PEACE in this
special little baby.

So, remember—**God has a way of making going around in circles a blessing.**

_____

_____

_____

_____

_____

_____

My Mama Was Two-Sided

I forgot to tell y'all:
Two always make one better...

As a child, it was a mystery watching my mama as she went about her motherly duties. I had questions in my mind, like...

- Where did she get that superpower?

- How did she accomplish so many things in so little time?

- When did she find time for herself to rest?

To me, it was fascinating how one woman could be more than one thing.
How could she be?

Strong yet gentle... Bold yet humble... Stern yet gracious... Boisterous yet calming...

Oh, how she amazed me!

How did she manage to meet all the needs of the home while working and nurturing, day after day? I often wondered why she would spend so much time in the closet. I wondered what she was doing in there. Some days, she would be in there longer than others, and at times, I could hear her talking and humming—

sometimes even weeping. But when she came out, she was...

- More gentle

- More humble

- More gracious

- More calming

It was like the closet was a refuge for her—a place in the home only she knew about, a place where she went in to be **RESTORED** and **PREPARED** for all the tasks she would have to complete.

Because I found At that time, I could only imagine what went on in that closet. But now that some people call me *Mama*, I've found out why my mama would go into the closet...

mine. I found my closet.

What If...

I forgot to tell y'all!
If we don't complete the task, we risk the failure of all connected.

Do you ever think about the daily tasks that are before you each day? You know, the simple things, like... getting dressed, preparing for work, making sure our kids are ready for school, and don't forget dinner.

As important as these tasks are in our daily lives, we shouldn't neglect the tasks we have in this journey of life with Christ.

Don't forget to acknowledge...
***God*... with PRAYER, PRAISE & WORSHIP!!**
*Don't forget to **LOVE** and be **GENEROUS** to all mankind!!*
*Don't forget to spread the **JOY of the LORD!!** which brings **STRENGTH!!***
*Don't forget to show the **PEACE of God!!***
*That will surpass all **UNDERSTANDING!!***
*Don't forget to be **GENTLE and GOOD!!***
*Don't forget to stay **STRONG and COURAGEOUS!!** Fighting the good fight of **FAITH!!***

*What if we ignore all the things I mentioned above? We would risk all opportunities to show the **LOVE of CHRIST**...*

God is...
Our Who Dat!!

I forgot to tell y'all...
The Bible says... **God is!!**

So, who is He to you?
Let me let you in on a little secret... I promise I won't be long at all.

God is...
Alpha and Omega, which means He **starts** IT and He **finishes** IT—no matter what *IT* is.

God is…
The Author and Finisher of our Faith, which means even though He's written the story, we have to trust in Him **totally** and believe in Him. He has plans for us, and you know the plans are good… *The Bible says so!*

God is…
Our Refuge—He's our safe place when life gets out of control. We don't have to fear. He's our shelter. We don't have to starve—He's our bread. We don't have to thirst—He's our well, and He never runs dry… *The Bible says so!*

God is…
Our Counselor—He's our go-to when everyone else has failed us. **God is our lawyer**—though all kinds of situations come up, Jesus pleads on our behalf, and God forgives… God sets free… God cleans up… God restores… God

makes us whole again... *The Bible says so!*

God is...
Our Healer—when doctors have given up and medicine has failed us... Guess what? We have **stripes** that we didn't even earn, and those stripes represent the **healing power of Jesus**! Oh yeah—before I forget—we have the **blood of Jesus** that washes away all our sickness and disease... He did that on the cross for us... *The Bible says so!*

God is...
Love. Yes! And you know what **LOVE** is, and you know what **LOVE** does... I don't have to tell ya!

GOD SHOWED His LOVE through JESUS, and GOD CONTINUES to LOVE on US...

Ask me how I know?

We Belong

I forgot to tell y'all:
The EARTH is the Lord's, the WORLD, and we who dwell here.

Let me start by asking you a question:
Have you ever taken for granted that you are being kept?

So many things happen in the world today—natural disasters, violence, and, as we say... accidents waiting to happen. Yet, we are still here by grace. Even circumstances we have put ourselves in could have caused physical, mental, or even total destruction to our lives or the lives of others.

But God, in all of His **MAJESTY**, finds ways in His busy schedule to **PROTECT** us—even when we are not in a place of obedience to Him. He always has a loving heart and open arms toward us, slow to be angry with us. Even with Him being God, He alone can command and allow anything to happen.

Yet, He still gives us **GRACE** and **MERCY**, and He is **PATIENT** with us. Why, you ask? **Because we belong to Him.** You know how you feel when something or someone is a part of you—it's your treasure, your investment. And what do you do? You watch over it, protect it, and cherish it.

That's exactly what God does for us. His eye watches over us, He has a host of angels protecting us, and the **Holy Spirit** is a gift sent to teach and guide us into the will of God for our lives. You see, God has made a **GREAT investment** in you and me.

A question to ponder... **Are we living worthy of being invested in?**

_____

_____

_____

_____

_____

_____

_____

_____

Poor Little Rich Girl

I forgot to tell y'all:

Hidden deep inside is where your treasure is...

Once upon a time, there was a poor little rich girl who lived in a town where everyone was wealthy in goods. But this poor little rich girl had none of these items—no silver, no gold, or even fine linens to be told.

She wandered around town both day and night with nowhere to sleep and very little to eat. She would pray every night that God would make her like everyone else. Little did she know, she was made special and unique, and that inside her was where all her treasure was stored. All she had to do was open her mouth and, by faith, speak her heart's desires into existence.

This short tale is for us today. Don't walk around this earth wanting and needing when you already possess all the love, all the gifts, and all the talent you need. It's all within you. **You are the key** that unlocks the doors to your dreams. Always remember that **the power of life and death is in what we say.**

So, **speak LIFE!**
Don't walk around poor when your Heavenly Father is rich...

_____

_____

_____

_____

_____

_____

_____

_____

_____

_____

_____

Always Something...

I forgot to tell y'all:

YOU always have something; YOU can't ever have nothing without having something.

Do you ever wonder why we sometimes say, *I don't have anything*—when all the while, we always have something? Let me help you discover all that you have so you can stop the cycle of saying, *I don't have anything*.

- **YOU will always have** a kind word to say...

- **YOU will always have** a smile to give...

- **YOU will always have** a friendly hand to lend...

- **YOU will always have** a lesson to learn...

- **YOU will always have** a skill to teach...

- **YOU will always have** an opportunity to make someone else's day better...

You see, all you need to do is **tap into YOU**, and you will always discover that your possibilities of having something are **ENDLESS**.

Leading the Way

I forgot to tell y'all:

Winner takes all...

I'm pretty sure we have all experienced some dark places in our lives—places we never even imagined we would go, experiences we never thought we would encounter. But there we were, standing right smack in the middle of it.

Some of us probably just wandered around in the dark, not even reaching out for something or someone to help guide us through. Let's be honest—we get a little prideful in our situations and think we know it all, that we have all the answers, when honestly, we really don't know what to do.

Ask yourself a question: **Do I want to keep stumbling, falling, and wandering around in the dark, being silent and too ashamed to reach out for help?** Of course not! These moments can either **make or break you—or both.**

This can be a time of **refinement** for you—a time when you humbly submit all your cares and worries to God, allowing Him to download His plan and purpose for your life—**plans for peace, joy, and love.**

Remember, in your most difficult moments, **you still have victory in God**, and He is always there, waiting to deliver you, waiting to enjoy a relationship with you.

Now I Know...

I forgot to tell y'all:

We sometimes don't understand at that moment, but when revelation comes...

As a young girl, it was strange to me how I would sit in my room playing old gospel songs and recording myself singing on my tape recorder.

Songs like...
"For the Good of Them," "The Race Is Not Given to the Swift nor Strong," "My

Storage Is Empty," and *"I'm Available to You."*

I got so full this past week. You see, at that time, as a young girl, I didn't know those very songs would be a part of the **strength** I needed in tough times as an adult.

Music played a very important role in my life as a child. It **transformed my thoughts** and **changed my environment.** I'm sharing this because we should always be **mindful of what our children listen to**—and us as well.

Always remember: **What we put in is what will come out.**

_____

_____

_____

Always a Way Back

I forgot to tell y'all:

The PATHWAY may not always be what we expect...

Having children brings great expectations. We do everything we can to make sure they have all the things in life that will make them **HAPPY, HEALTHY, and SUCCESSFUL.** We would go to the ends of the earth for our children.

But what happens when their direction takes an unexpected turn?

The Word of God tells us to **direct our children in the pathway they should go,** but oftentimes, our children don't always follow our instructions. They create their own path in life—and that's okay. **As long as we follow the instructions given to us by God's Word, no matter what road they may choose, they won't forget the pathway you established for them.**

The best thing we can do as parents is to **remain in FAITH** and be there with open arms **when the path they chose ends… and the life God intended begins.**

High as a Kite...

I forgot to tell y'all:

I got a high that is higher than the highest height.

Take a second to think about this... Have you ever wondered why generations keep looking for things to make them high? And I'm not just talking about the people we see every day out in the streets getting their high...

Nooo... **You. Me. Too.**

We all get high off something—whether it be legal or illegal, we all have something we feel we need to **jump-start our start**—*and that could be the start of anything.*

Sometimes the addict is not just the one in the street...

- It's the one in the **CHURCH.**

- It's the one in the **GOVERNMENT.**

- It's the one in the **MOVIES.**

- It's the one in the **SCHOOLS.**

It's our **addictions** that keep us from an intimate moment with the **MOST HIGH** we could ever know... You know...

- The ONE who SAVES.

- The ONE who RULES.

- The ONE who LOVES.

- The ONE who TEACHES.

And it is **HIS WILL** that we put no other gods (addictions) before HIM!

Be mindful: **An addiction is anything we put before GOD... anything we feel we need more than GOD.**

I Don't Get Paid to Do That...

I forgot to tell y'all:

Hard work and sacrifice come with DUTY...

Question: Have you ever heard the words, *"That's not my job"* or *"I don't* *get paid to do that'*? Do you ever find yourself saying those exact words sometimes?

Perhaps when we are on our jobs, most of the time, we go in with the mindset of... *I'm doing my part and nothing else. I don't get paid to do all that.* Come on, let's be real about it. For some of us, that becomes our way of living. But are we really living when we think like that?

We all have roles to play in life. For example, I'm a mom, but I can't just tell my child, *Look, I'm only your mother and nothing else.* Then, when something unexpected happens—like my child falling off a bicycle—what will I do? Just stand there and say, *I'm just your mother and that's it—nothing else*? No! I will run to my child and...

- Comfort them (**counselor**)

- Aid any bruises or cuts (**nurse**)

- Tell them, *"It's okay, you can try again"* (**encourager**)

In that moment, I become more than just a mother. I'm a counselor, a nurse, and an encourager. I can't say, *Oh, I'm just your mom here to feed you and that's it.* No, I have other duties that must be done.

As Christians, we should not have the mindset of... *I go to church, get my word, and go—nothing else.* No! Of course, go and get God's word, but don't keep it to yourself. Don't limit yourself to just that. The Bible says we must spread the word all over the earth, compelling men to follow Christ.

LISTEN... We have work to do, and we may have to put in some overtime, BUT guess what...

WE ALREADY GOT PAID!!!

JESUS is the only ONE who can say, *"I did ONE thing and nothing else."* And that ONE thing **COVERED IT ALL.**

It's Okay to...
BE-the-WORD

I forgot to tell y'all:

Relax. It's okay to just BE-YOU!

- **BE** anxious for nothing—wait on the Lord...

- **BE** angry, but don't sin—pray without ceasing...

- **BE** holy, for He is holy—obey the voice of God and do...

- **BE** transformed by a renewed mind—concentrate, keep straight ahead, ignore all distractions...

- **BE** vigilant—focus your attention on things above, not on this earth...

- **BE** strong in the Lord—fight the good fight...

- **BE** willing and obedient—eat the good of the land...

- **BE** faithful in small beginnings—rule later over plenty...

- **BE** loved—love one another, for love comes from GOD, and GOD is love...

- **BE** like CHRIST—humble yourself, give, and it will **BE** given back, measurably...

Now you see, it's all good to... **BE-the-Word.**

In Moments Like These

I forgot to tell y'all:
It will be in a moment, before you can even blink your eyes...

We all have moments we would love to enjoy again and also moments we just don't want to revisit. The most popular moments, I believe, are the ones we would love to relive—those filled with fun and laughter among friends and family.

Don't you think those are the most precious moments?

Fun, family, and laughter bring so much joy to your heart, to the point where, every time you think about those moments, you smile and remember how precious they made you feel inside.

Then, there are moments we would love to forget—moments we want to disappear, never to return again. Moments when we've felt pain, disappointment, and despair. But would you be super upset with me if I told you that those moments—when we feel or experience the worst of things—are the most important moments we could ever have in this lifetime?

These are the moments when you finally realize who truly loves you, no matter what's going on in your life. The moments when you finally understand that you can't do anything alone in your own strength. The moments when the tears become unbearable, and you've almost lost all faith and hope in everything.

And then—**in one moment, before you can even blink your eyes—God steps in.**

He restores you back to life, waking up all the dead things and bringing you back to a life filled with joy, peace, and happiness like none other.

So, before I forget to tell y'all:
These are your testimony moments…

_____

_____

Knock, Knock, Knock

I forgot to tell y'all:
We are never totally alone... there is always a door open for us...

Matthew 7:7
"Ask and it will be given to you; seek and you will find; knock and the door will be opened to you."

Ever tried visiting someone who said they would be home, but upon your arrival, they were not there? The door was locked, and you had no key to enter—only questions.

Where could the owner of the home be? Why did they invite you over to an empty house?

In the meantime, most of us would probably knock a few more times or look through the front windows, making sure no one was home before turning around and heading toward the car.

But what if I told you about this door I heard about—a door that's never locked, always open, and the access to enter is found in you? Yes, you!

God has given you all access to an open door that never revolves. You can enter in, be greeted with love, and be well cared for. Everything you want and need—all of your heart's desires—can be fulfilled when you walk through this door. All you need to do is… ask, seek, and knock.

It's never empty inside this door—someone is always home.

Oh, before I forget to tell you...

YOU WILL NEVER, EVER HAVE TO WORRY ABOUT IF HE'S HOME, BECAUSE HIS INVITATION IS ALWAYS VALID, AND YOU ARE ALWAYS WELCOME.

And one more thing... **YOU CAN PLAN ON STAYING FOREVER.**

_____

_____

_____

_____

_____

_____

You Have Your Mother's Strength...

You have your mother's **STRENGTH**
If you're riding the difficult waves of life.

You have your mother's **STRENGTH**
If the pain you feel is unbearable.

You have your mother's **STRENGTH**
If loneliness wants to become your best friend.

You have your mother's **STRENGTH**
If being misunderstood causes irritation.

You have your mother's **STRENGTH**
If being disappointed causes you grief.

You have your mother's **STRENGTH**
If life gets unmanageable and you feel like giving up.

You have your mother's **STRENGTH**
If you remember the **LOVE** she has for you.

You have your mother's **STRENGTH**
If you can still hear her words of **WISDOM**.

You have your mother's **STRENGTH**
If you embrace the **PEACE** of **GOD** and allow it to **SUPERSEDE** your **UNDERSTANDING**.

Just a reminder to you today: Your mother's strength was in **GOD**, and **YOU ARE YOUR MOTHER'S STRENGTH.**

SO STAND STRONG.

_____

_____

_____

_____

_____

_____

_____

_____

_____

I Promise
I Won't Be Long...

I forgot to tell y'all:
Patience is a virtue, but time is of the essence...

Do you remember being very young and maybe a little scared when it was time for Mom and Dad to go to work, and they had to drop you off at daycare? You would hear the words, *"Don't worry, I won't be long, I promise."*

But as a young child, you didn't really understand time or how long it would take before you saw Mom and Dad again. All you knew was that you were in this unfamiliar place, looking at and being seen by people you didn't know.

Throughout the day, frustration would set in, along with anxiety—not knowing when your parents would arrive to save you from this unfamiliar place and these unfamiliar faces.

Then, a little hope arrived—a teacher came along and showed you toys, games, and books. She shared and taught you different ways to handle the separation from your parents. And then, before you could even blink your eyes, there they were—Mom and Dad, as promised.

Jesus made us promises too—that He will be coming back for us. We do not fully understand or know His timing, but in the meantime, He left us a **Teacher** in the **Holy Spirit**—here to lead, guide, and show us ways to occupy our time until that **GREAT DAY** when **JESUS** returns for us.

_____

_____

_____

_____

_____

_____

_____

_____

The Good New Days...

I forgot to tell y'all:

- Better days are promised, reminding us to hold on to **hope**, knowing that God's **goodness** will prevail.

I know we all have heard people say, *"Those were the good old days."*

But did you also know that God has promised us **GOOD NEW DAYS?**

The **GOOD NEW DAYS** God has promised are not only for when He returns—we are in **GOOD DAYS** now...

When God **WAKES** us up in the morning—that's a **GOOD DAY**...
When God **MEETS** all our needs—that's a **GOOD DAY**...
When God **PROTECTS** us from danger—that's a **GOOD DAY**...
When God **PROVIDES** food on our table—that's a **GOOD DAY**...
When God **HEALS** us from all sickness and disease—that's a **GOOD DAY**...

So, the next time you're in a conversation with someone and they say, *"Those were the good old days,"* remind them that we are living in some **GOOD NEW DAYS**.

Remind them of God's PROMISES.

I Can Care Less...

I forgot to tell y'all:
My relationship with God has made such a difference in my life—to the point where I just don't care.

I can care less...
When I am weary.

I can care less...
When I am mistreated.

I can care less...
When I am rejected.

I can care less...
When I am lied on.

I can care less...
When I am talked about.

I can care less...
When fear tries to discourage me.

I can care less...
When sickness tries to destroy me.

I can care less...
When loneliness tries to distance me.

Why should I care about these things?

When I am...
the HEAD and not the TAIL...
When I am...
ABOVE only and not beneath...
When I am...
more than a CONQUEROR through JESUS...

When I am TRUSTING and OBEYING GOD's WORD...

NONE of these things MOVE me.

Because GOD is my...
ROCK when I am weary.
COMFORT when I am sad.
STRENGTH when I am weak.

You see, I GAVE all of my cares to GOD because He cares MORE...

So, I can care less...

_____

_____

_____

_____

_____

I'll Take
the Leftovers...

I forgot to tell y'all:
Leftovers are always better as time goes on.

Remember when Mom cooked that special meal, and we all sat at the table and ate to our heart's content? But Mom would always say, *"It will be even better tomorrow when all the seasonings set in."*

It's the same with our walk with God. As we accept our salvation and begin to allow Jesus to become Lord over our lives, some simmering begins—just like in cooking. And one of the main ingredients Jesus left for us is His **PEACE**.

John 14:27 (NIV)
"Peace I leave with you; my peace I give you. I do not give to you as the world gives. Do not let your hearts be troubled and do not be afraid."

You see, acknowledging and accepting that Jesus left His **PEACE** for us is all we need to endure uncertain times. We don't have to worry or fret because of the **PEACE** of God.

PEACE that surpasses all understanding... *Philippians 4:7*
We are blessed when we become **PEACEmakers**... *Matthew 5:9*
God's covenant of **PEACE** shall always remain... *Isaiah 54:10*

STRENGTH is found in God's **PEACE**...
Psalm 29:11
Sowing **PEACE** reaps a harvest of **RIGHTEOUSNESS**... *James 3:18*
PEACE keeps us in unity with God's Spirit... *Ephesians 4:3*

Don't YOU want what God left for us?

Don't just accept and acknowledge **PEACE**—every day, we should make every effort not only to live in **PEACE** but to spread **PEACE** to EVERYONE.

Life gets better when we allow **PEACE** to set in...

_____
_____
_____
_____

Sorry, We're Closed...

I forgot to tell y'all:
Sometimes, closure is a wonderful thing...

Ever pulled up to your favorite store or restaurant, only to see a sign that read **"Sorry, We're Closed"** with no explanation? I have, and I wondered why there was no notice. I thought to myself, *"They could have at least said something to the public, right?"*

In that case, yes, we feel disappointed when our favorite store or restaurant shuts down without warning.

Oh well, we have to move on and find new favorites.

But I'm saying all that to say this: It's time for us to **shut down** and serve notice to some issues (**sin**) in our lives. It's time to shut the enemy down in areas where he's been putting things on sale and adding to the menu of our lives.

I challenge you, as we begin the holiday season and enter a new year, to develop a checklist of things you want closure on—things you want to eliminate and shut down in your life.

It's time for a fresh, new you! Begin now, so when January 1, 2025, comes, it's not just your **New Year's RESOLUTION**—it's your **LIFESTYLE**.

I Had No Clue...

I forgot to tell y'all:
Don't panic! Sometimes in **LIFE**, we just don't have any idea... and that's okay.

Remember when you were wandering around this planet, searching for something, but didn't know exactly what you were searching for?

At first, you thought it was in a person—only to find out that wasn't it. Then, you thought you could find it in your education or career—but no, it wasn't there either.

Here we are, still wandering, still waiting for that one thing that will bring that **JOY**... that **PEACE**... that **HAPPINESS** we all long for—only to find out it's not in a person or a career.

It's wonderful to have good people in our lives and successful careers, but it doesn't start or stop there. That's not our **FIRM FOUNDATION**.

DISCOVERING and **MAINTAINING** a TRUE, COMMITTED RELATIONSHIP with **JESUS** will end all the wandering you're experiencing. **JESUS** has all the ideas you need— more than you can even think or imagine.

So, don't worry if you just don't have a **CLUE** in this **LIFE**. I'll share one **CLUE** that helped me during my wandering...

I wandered around and found something in **Jeremiah 29:11**—there are some **GOOD PLANS** there, and **GREAT EXPECTATIONS** await...

_____

_____

_____

_____

_____

_____

_____

_____

_____

GodzGirl InspireOne...

She's **ZEALOUS**, showing great energy (**FAITH**) and enthusiasm (**EXCITEMENT**) in pursuit of her cause, her objective, her **PURPOSE**.

She lives the **Zoe Life**
(A **FULL LIFE** with **GOD**)

GodzGirl is that girl... that lady... that woman...

She's mistreated.
She's misunderstood.

She's been violated.
She's violent.
She's angry.
She's confused.
She's secretive.
She's trapped.
She's free.
She's weak.
She's strong.
She's a wife.
She's a mom.
She's a daughter.
She's a sister.
She's a friend.
She's lost.
She's saved.
She's educated.
She's anointed.
She's superwoman.
She loves.
She hates.
She smiles.
She cries.

She gossips.
She speaks wisdom.

She is **GodZealousGirl**!

GodzGirl embodies the collective essence of all women.

We become **GodzGirl** when we grasp the profound reality of God's love for us—reassuring us that regardless of our past actions or words, we remain **God's beloved daughters**.

In my most despairing moment, when I felt lost and disconnected, God's soothing voice spoke directly to my heart. **GodzGirl** became my safe haven, my motivation, and my inspiration.

She gave me the strength to forgive myself for past errors and begin a life of purpose, driven by a singular passion: **to love, honor, and obey God, allowing Him to always guide and protect me.**

Acknowledging the vastness of God's love for us **triggers transformations** in every area of our lives—making all else **secondary** to the primary goal of **pleasing God and inspiring others.**

I encourage you to **let go of your past**, for a **promising future** is ahead of you.

GodzGirl, it is time to InspireOne...

_____

_____

_____

_____

Red Means Go...
and Break the Rules...

I forgot to tell y'all: Because of RED, you are free to GO!!

It's such a PRIVILEGE to have a driver's license and go wherever you want, anytime, any day. But with all the PRIVILEGE of having a driver's license, there are still RULES we must follow—like being mindful of our speed and knowing when to turn our blinkers on so that others will know if we're turning left or right. We must also know when to apply our brakes so we don't RUN into people. Oh yes, then there are the traffic lights—red symbolizing STOP, yellow for CAUTION, and green to GO.

But... I want to let you in on something I found out—something that will help you realize that the color RED doesn't always mean STOP. In fact, it can actually allow you to GO and BREAK some RULES.

TRUST ME—you will LOVE ME for this ONE...

JESUS BROKE all the RULES when He traveled to Calvary. Actually, He ignored them just so that we could be free to live this LIFE of FREEDOM. He TRAVELED down the streets, carrying our heavy load, ignoring all stop signs. He didn't use signals to turn left or right—He steadily kept moving forward. I'm sure He had distractions, but He was determined to reach His destination for us.

The BLOOD OF JESUS BROKE all the RULES of BONDAGE, and we are no longer slaves to unrighteousness. RED, for us, actually means GO!!

GO RUNNING into people, traveling the streets all over the earth, telling everyone that all RULES of BONDAGE have been BROKEN because of RED.

The BLOOD of JESUS has set us FREE!! NO MORE BONDAGE!!

LET PEOPLE KNOW!

JESUS BROKE the RULES and led us to PRIVILEGES!!

Dress Accordingly...

I forgot to tell y'all:
Prepare! I hear the weather may not be favorable—you need to make sure you're **protected**.

Every day, we check the weather report because we want to know the forecast. Some of us even need to know what the weather will be for the rest of the week. We do this because we want to know what to wear and how to prepare for whatever the day may bring.

If **RAIN** is predicted, we need our **UMBRELLA** to **PROTECT** us from getting wet. If the weather is expected to be extremely **COLD**, we need our **COATS** to **PROTECT** us from the chilly air. If the **SUN** is said to **SHINE BRIGHT,** we need to **WEAR** clothing that will keep us **COOL** and **DRY.**

In the **KINGDOM OF GOD**, there are **ELEMENTS** we need so that we are **EQUIPPED** and **READY** for whatever conditions **LIFE** may bring. The **WORD OF GOD** prepares us for the challenges of **LIFE** by reminding us to put on...

- The **BELT OF TRUTH** buckled around your waist

- The **BREASTPLATE OF RIGHTEOUSNESS**

- Our **FEET FITTED** with the readiness that comes from the **GOSPEL OF PEACE**

- The **SHIELD OF FAITH**, with which you can extinguish all the flaming arrows of the evil one

- The **HELMET OF SALVATION**

- The **SWORD OF THE SPIRIT**, which is the **WORD OF GOD**

- And **PRAY IN THE SPIRIT OF GOD** on **ALL OCCASIONS**

I guarantee that if we stay **READY** and **EQUIPPED**, we will be prepared for **ALL CONDITIONS OF LIFE.**

_____

_____

For Mature Adults Only...

This Film Has Not Been Rated... Yet.

I forgot to tell y'all:
The camera is always rolling... the dress rehearsal is real.

Question:

1. Do you like working behind the scenes?

2. Do you prefer being out on the stage where everyone can see you?

The answer to each question is so vital to the ending of the story.

Let's ponder on question one. Working behind the scenes requires you to stay ready—asserting, assisting, and encouraging the actors. Assisting the director of the movie with any and every assignment.
You are always **busy, busy,** making yourself available, with no time for yourself, it seems. But you are in the presence of the director always, and there are moments between filming to take a break...

What are you doing on your break? Because what you do on break will count at the end of the movie. **Use the time wisely!!!**

Question two:
Do you prefer being out on stage, performing for the crowd? Now,

that's a good one. The thing about this question is that most of the time, you are pretending to be someone else. Be careful with this opportunity, because you have to be **fake**—but keep in mind, it's for entertainment purposes only. Try not to **lose** yourself in character along the way; that can be dangerous.

If in doubt about any behavior you're faced with or feel uncomfortable with, seek out the director of the movie. I'm pretty sure you'll find solutions there.

Finally, if you take the time during rehearsal and filming to seek the director for guidance... I'm sure you will do a good job, and you will see your name as they roll the credits at the end of the movie.

There's a
New Dance in Town...

I forgot to tell y'all:

Dances come and dances go, but this new **dance** has you in the **RIGHT** place, at the **RIGHT** time, dancing to the **RIGHT** tune.

Remember when you were growing up, and there was always a **NEW DANCE** to learn? Like breakdancing, the electric boogaloo, and that famous dance everyone does at the end of every wedding or party—the **LINE DANCE**.

When learning to dance, you want to make sure your arms, feet, and body are making the **RIGHT** moves, so you practice and practice until you get it **RIGHT**.

Then the **BIG DAY** comes when all your friends and all the neighborhood kids come out, gathering in one **SPOT** to see who has learned the exact moves of how this **NEW DANCE** goes. Everyone is all hyped up and excited, ready to see who will win the dance competition.

You have **practiced** hard on this one thing, and you would love to win and achieve the title of being the best dancer around town.

I know—the thought of it all makes you feel happy inside.

But let me take a moment and share with you how this **NEW DANCE** goes... First of all, the **CREATOR** of this **NEW DANCE** would love to dance along with you at every event, making sure you know all the **RIGHT** moves—never missing a beat. And when the two of you are dancing together, you will have **HAPPY FEELINGS** inside.

Before I forget to tell you, the title of this **NEW DANCE** is **STEPPING INTO THE RIGHT DIRECTION**...

YOU don't need to worry—there is still a little time left. But no one knows exactly how much time, so if I were you, I would get in that **LINE** before it's too late...

Today would be the perfect day...

I heard there are some **SPOTS** open. People will be gathering together, especially those who would love to learn the moves to...

The NEW DANCE that's in town...

_____
_____
_____
_____
_____
_____
_____
_____

Author Contact Page

For permission requests, inquiries, or bulk orders, contact: godzgirlinspireone@gmail.com

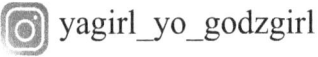 Christ Producing Restoration

  yagirl_yo_godzgirl

www.ingramcontent.com/pod-product-compliance
Lightning Source LLC
Chambersburg PA
CBHW060031180426
43196CB00044B/2372